JOHN THOMPSON'S
EASIEST PIANO COURSE

FIRST CHART HITS

3	**Stay**	RIHANNA
6	**Roar**	KATY PERRY
10	**All of Me**	JOHN LEGEND
14	**Home**	PHILLIP PHILLIPS
18	**Let Her Go**	PASSENGER
22	**Love Runs Out**	ONEREPUBLIC
26	**Cups (When I'm Gone)**	ANNA KENDRICK
28	**Happy**	PHARRELL

ISBN 978-1-4950-0918-1

WILLIS MUSIC

Exclusively Distributed By

HAL•LEONARD®
CORPORATION

© 2014 by The Willis Music Co.
International Copyright Secured   All Rights Reserved

For all works contained herein:
Unauthorized copying, arranging, adapting, recording, Internet posting, public performance,
or other distribution of the printed music in this publication is an infringement of copyright.
Infringers are liable under the law.

Visit Hal Leonard Online at
www.halleonard.com

Teachers and Parents

This collection of popular songs, arranged in the John Thompson tradition,
is intended as supplementary material for the later elementary pianist. The pieces may also be
used for sight-reading practice by more advanced students.

Stay

Words and Music by Mikky Ekko
and Justin Parker

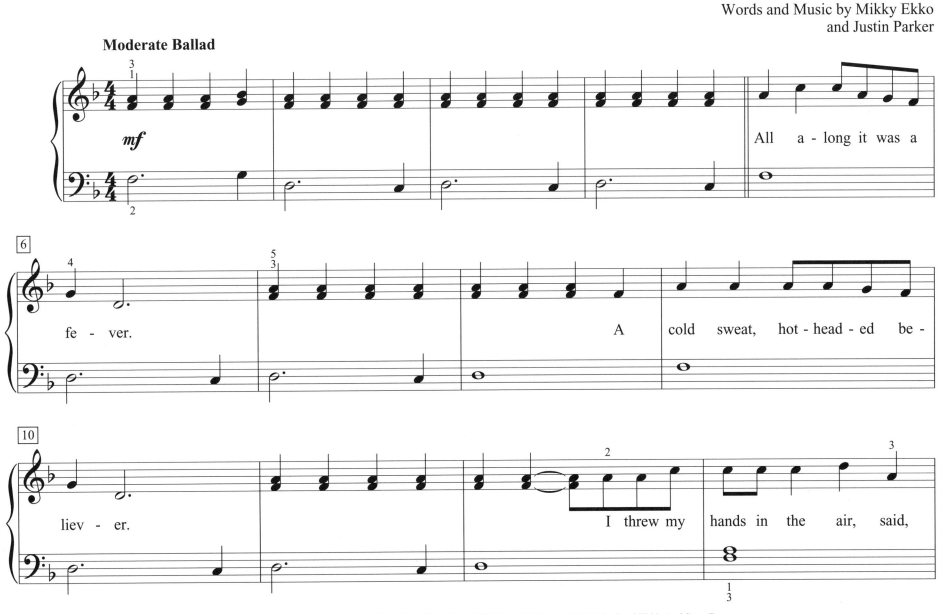

Copyright © 2012 Sony/ATV Music Publishing LLC, Sony/ATV Music Publishing UK Limited and Kkids And Stray Dogs
This arrangement Copyright © 2014 Sony/ATV Music Publishing LLC, Sony/ATV Music Publishing UK Limited and Kkids And Stray Dogs
All Rights Administered by Sony/ATV Music Publishing LLC, 424 Church Street, Suite 1200, Nashville, TN 37219
International Copyright Secured   All Rights Reserved

4

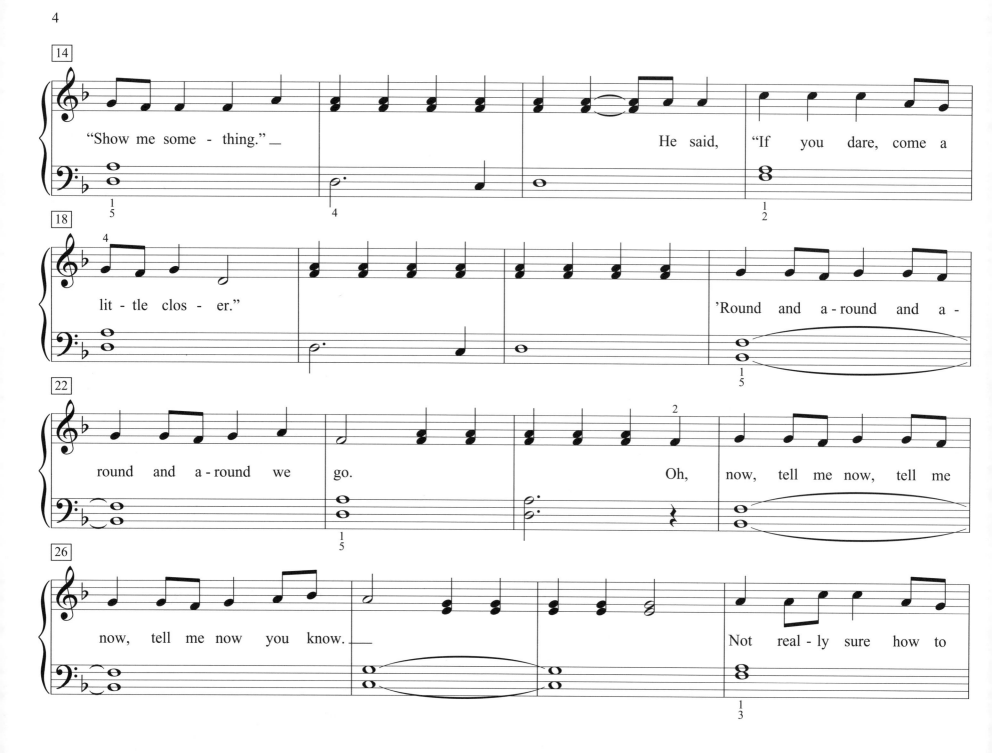

Roar

Words and Music by Katy Perry,
Lukasz Gottwald, Max Martin,
Bonnie McKee and Henry Walter

© 2013 WB MUSIC CORP., WHEN I'M RICH YOU'LL BE MY B**CH, SONGS OF PULSE RECORDING, PRESCRIPTION SONGS,
BONNIE McKEE MUSIC, WHERE DA KASZ AT?, MXM MUSIC AB, KASZ MONEY PUBLISHING and ONEIROLOGY PUBLISHING
This arrangement © 2014 WB MUSIC CORP., WHEN I'M RICH YOU'LL BE MY B**CH, SONGS OF PULSE RECORDING, PRESCRIPTION SONGS,
BONNIE McKEE MUSIC, WHERE DA KASZ AT?, MXM MUSIC AB, KASZ MONEY PUBLISHING and ONEIROLOGY PUBLISHING
All Rights for WHEN I'M RICH YOU'LL BE MY B**CH Administered by WB MUSIC CORP.
All Rights for SONGS OF PULSE RECORDING Administered by DOWNTOWN DMP SONGS/DOWNTOWN MUSIC PUBLISHING LLC
All Rights for PRESCRIPTION SONGS, MXM MUSIC AB, KASZ MONEY PUBLISHING and ONEIROLOGY PUBLISHING Administered by KOBALT SONGS MUSIC PUBLISHING
All Rights for BONNIE McKEE MUSIC and WHERE DA KASZ AT? Administered by SONGS OF KOBALT MUSIC PUBLISHING
All Rights Reserved   Used by Permission

All of Me

Words and Music by John Stephens
and Toby Gad

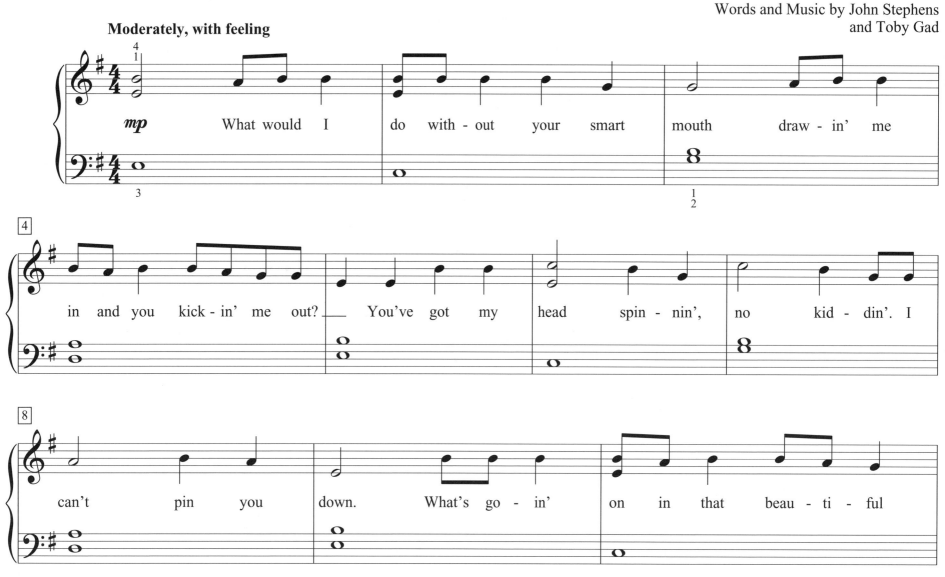

Copyright © 2013 John Legend Publishing, EMI April Music Inc. and Gad Songs, LLC
This arrangement Copyright © 2014 John Legend Publishing, EMI April Music Inc. and Gad Songs, LLC
All Rights for John Legend Publishing Administered by BMG Rights Management (US) LLC
All Rights for EMI April Music Inc. and Gad Songs, LLC Administered by Sony/ATV Music Publishing LLC, 424 Church Street, Suite 1200, Nashville, TN 37219
All Rights Reserved   Used by Permission

Home

Words and Music by Greg Holden
and Drew Pearson

Copyright © 2011, 2012 Fallen Art Music, Drewyeah Music and CYP Two Publishing
This arrangement Copyright © 2014 Fallen Art Music, Drewyeah Music and CYP Two Publishing
All Rights for Fallen Art Music Administered by Songs Of Razor & Tie d/b/a Razor & Tie Music Publishing, LLC
All Rights for Drewyeah Music and CYP Two Publishing Administered by Downtown DMP Songs/Downtown Music Publishing LLC
All Rights Reserved   Used by Permission

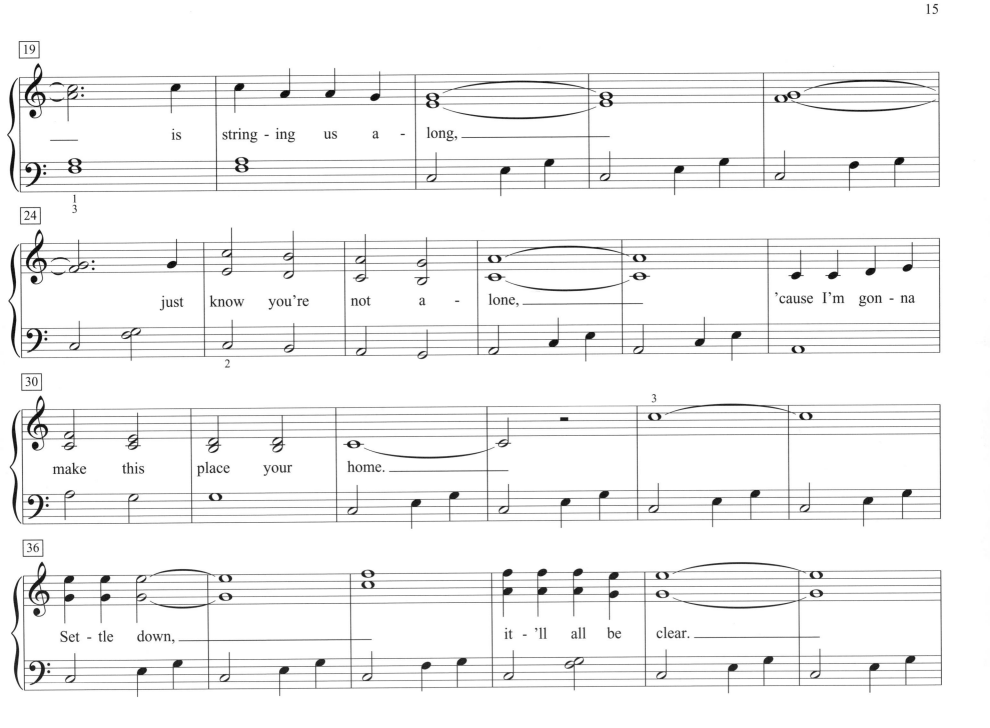

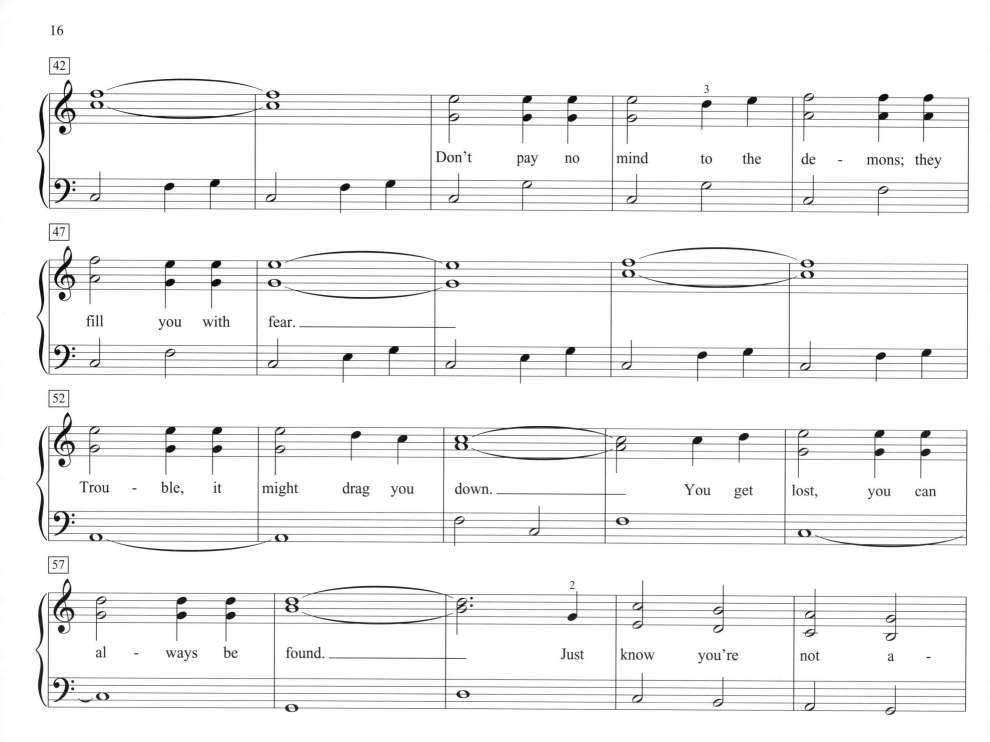

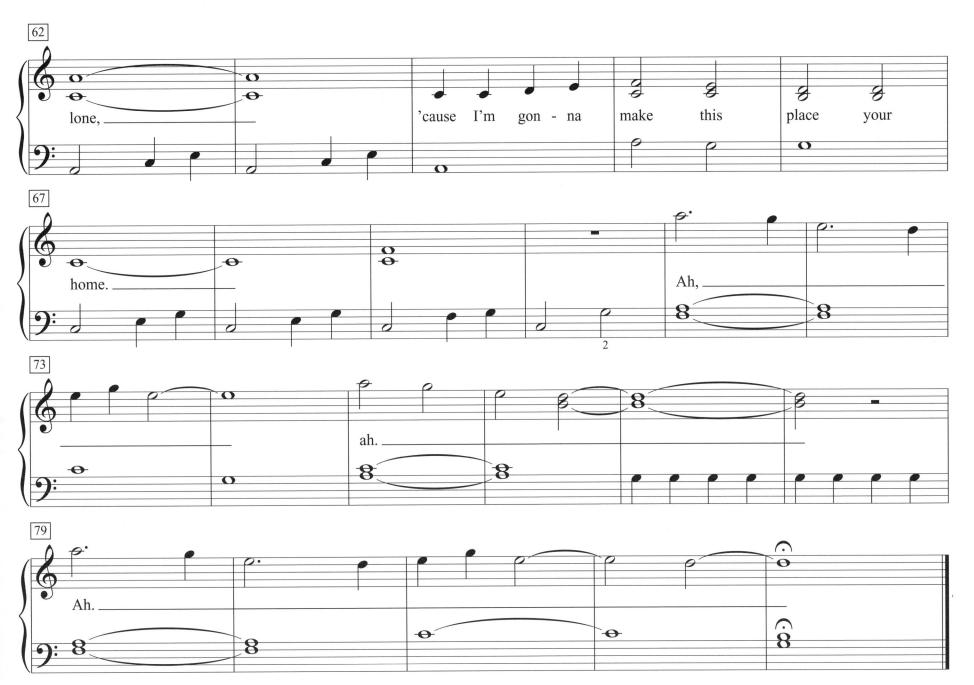

Let Her Go

Words and Music by
Michael David Rosenberg

Copyright © 2012 Sony/ATV Music Publishing (UK) Limited
This arrangement Copyright © 2014 Sony/ATV Music Publishing (UK) Limited
All Rights Administered by Sony/ATV Music Publishing LLC, 424 Church Street, Suite 1200, Nashville, TN 37219
International Copyright Secured   All Rights Reserved

And you let her go. ____

Star - ing at the bot - tom of your glass, hop - ing one day you'll make a dream last. But dreams come slow and they go so ____ fast.

Love Runs Out

Words and Music by Ryan Tedder,
Brent Kutzle, Zachary Filkins,
Eddie Fisher and Andrew Brown

Copyright © 2014 Sony/ATV Music Publishing LLC, Velvet Hammer Music, Midnite Miracle Music and Patriot Games Publishing
This arrangement Copyright © 2014 Sony/ATV Music Publishing LLC, Velvet Hammer Music, Midnite Miracle Music and Patriot Games Publishing
All Rights on behalf of Sony/ATV Music Publishing LLC, Velvet Hammer Music and Midnite Miracle Music Administered by Sony/ATV Music Publishing LLC, 424 Church Street, Suite 1200, Nashville, TN 37219
All Rights on behalf of Patriot Games Publishing Administered by Kobalt Songs Music Publishing
International Copyright Secured   All Rights Reserved

a fire and we'll shut it down 'til the love runs out, 'til the love_

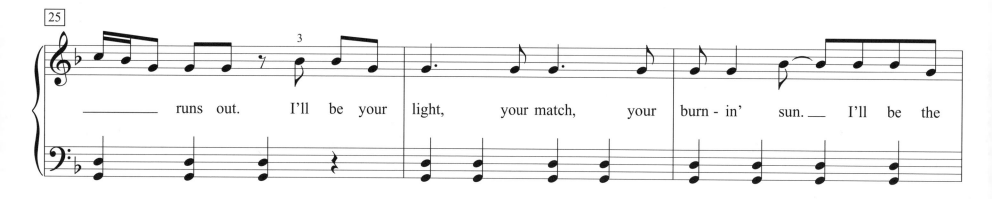

_____ runs out. I'll be your light, your match, your burn - in' sun._ I'll be the

bright in black that's mak - in' you run._ And we'll feel_____ al - right and we'll feel_

al - right 'cause we'll work it out, yeah, we'll work it out. And we'll start

a fire and we'll shut it down 'til the love runs out, 'til the love

runs out, 'til the love _____ runs ___ out. _____

Cups
(When I'm Gone)
from the Motion Picture Soundtrack PITCH PERFECT

Words and Music by A.P. Carter,
Luisa Gerstein and Heloise Tunstall-Behrens

Copyright © 2013 by Peer International Corporation and BMG Gold Songs
This arrangement Copyright © 2014 by Peer International Corporation and BMG Gold Songs
All Rights for BMG Gold Songs Administered by BMG Rights Management (US) LLC
International Copyright Secured   All Rights Reserved
- contains a sample from "When I'm Gone" by A.P. Carter

Happy

from DESPICABLE ME 2

Words and Music by
Pharrell Williams

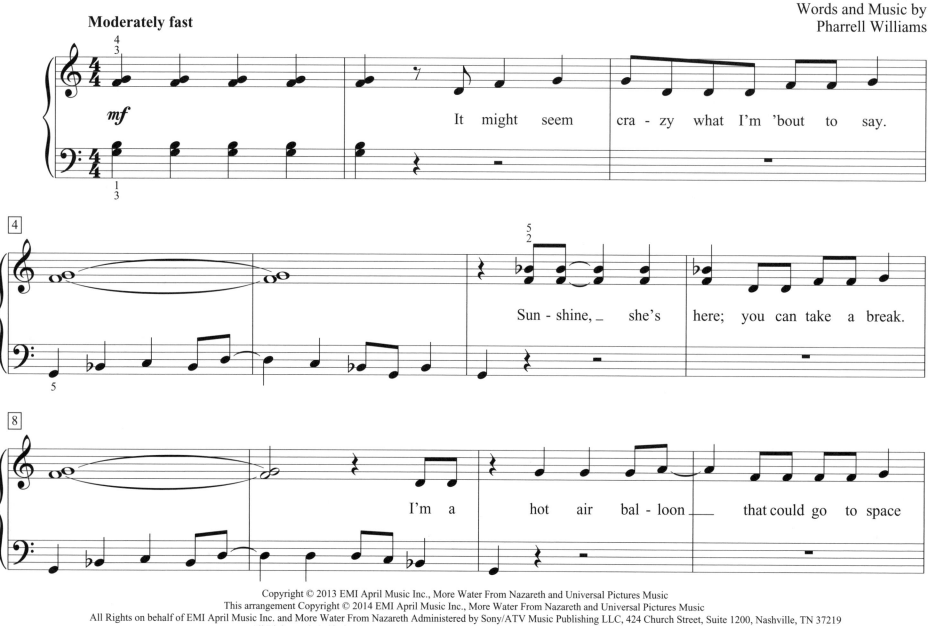

Copyright © 2013 EMI April Music Inc., More Water From Nazareth and Universal Pictures Music
This arrangement Copyright © 2014 EMI April Music Inc., More Water From Nazareth and Universal Pictures Music
All Rights on behalf of EMI April Music Inc. and More Water From Nazareth Administered by Sony/ATV Music Publishing LLC, 424 Church Street, Suite 1200, Nashville, TN 37219
All Rights on behalf of Universal Pictures Music Controlled and Administered by Universal Music Corp.
International Copyright Secured All Rights Reserved

with the air like I don't care, ba - by, by the way. ____

Huh! ____ (Be - cause I'm hap - py. ____
Clap a - long

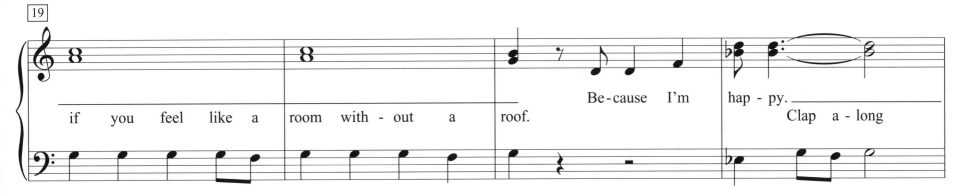

if you feel like a room with - out a roof. Be - cause I'm hap - py. ____
Clap a - long

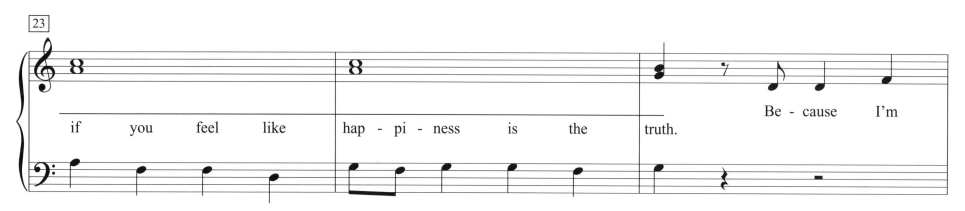

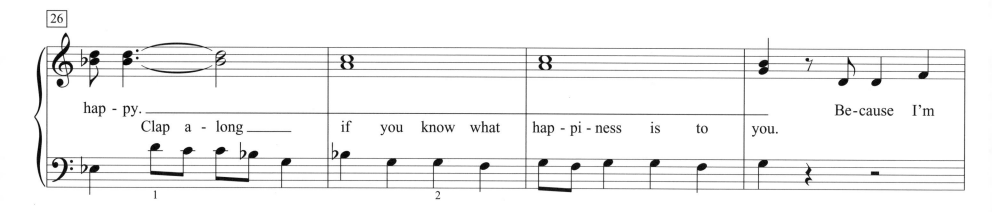

JOHN THOMPSON'S
EASIEST PIANO COURSE

Fun repertoire books now available as an integral part of **John Thompson's Easiest Piano Course...** Graded to work alongside the course, these pieces are ideal for pupils reaching the end of the beginning level. They are invaluable for securing basic technique as well as developing musicality and enjoyment.

John Thompson's Easiest Piano Course

00414014 Part 1 – Book only $4.99
00414018 Part 2 – Book only $5.99
00414019 Part 3 – Book only $5.99
00414112 Part 4 – Book only $5.99

John Thompson's First Christmas Duets

00416871 .... $7.99

John Thompson's First Classics

00406347 .... $4.95

John Thompson's First Disney Songs

00416880 .... $7.99

John Thompson's First Favorites

00406431 .... $4.95

John Thompson's First Folk Songs

00406243 .... $4.95

John Thompson's First Piano Duets

00406230 .... $4.95

EXCLUSIVELY DISTRIBUTED BY

HAL•LEONARD® CORPORATION

7777 W. BLEUMOUND RD. P.O. BOX 13819 MILWAUKEE, WI 53213

Also available from John Thompson:

First Christmas Tunes
00406426 .... $4.95

First Nursery Rhymes
00406229 .... $4.99

Prices, contents and availability subject to change without notice.

TEACHING LITTLE FINGERS TO PLAY

JOHN THOMPSON'S MODERN COURSE FOR THE PIANO

TEACHING LITTLE FINGERS TO PLAY

A BOOK FOR THE EARLIEST BEGINNER
COMBINING ROTE & NOTE APPROACH
"SOMETHING NEW IN EVERY LESSON"

W.M. Co. 5639

THE WILLIS MUSIC COMPANY
FLORENCE, KENTUCKY 41042

TEACHING LITTLE FINGERS TO PLAY
SONGS FROM MANY LANDS
International Songs for the Earliest Beginner
Arranged by Carolyn C. Setliff
THE WILLIS MUSIC COMPANY

TEACHING LITTLE FINGERS TO PLAY
EASY DUETS
Equal-Level Duets for Early Beginners
Arranged by Carolyn Miller
THE WILLIS MUSIC COMPANY

TEACHING LITTLE FINGERS TO PLAY
DISNEY TUNES
Delightful Disney Songs for the Earliest Beginner
Arranged by Glenda Austin
THE WILLIS MUSIC COMPANY

Disney characters and artwork are © Disney Enterprises, Inc.

TEACHING LITTLE FINGERS TO PLAY

A method for the early beginner combining rote and note approach. The melodies are written with careful thought and are kept as simple as possible, yet they are refreshingly delightful. All the music lies within the grasp of a child's small hands.

00412076	Book only	$4.99
00406523	Book/CD	$9.99

Foreign Language Editions

00414478	Book only (Spanish)	$4.99
00414498	Book only (French)	$4.95
00416444	Book only (Chinese)	$5.95

SUPPLEMENTARY SERIES

All books are at the early elementary level and include optional teacher accompaniments.

CHILDREN'S SONGS
arr. Carolyn Miller

10 familiar melodies: "C" is for Cookie • Elmo's Song • The Hokey Pokey • How Much is that Doggie in the Window • On Top of Spaghetti • Puff the Magic Dragon • and more.

00416808	Book only	$6.99
00416809	Book/CD	$12.99

CHRISTMAS FAVORITES
arr. Eric Baumgartner

9 songs celebrating the season: Blue Christmas • The Chipmunk Song • Do You Hear What I Hear • I'll Be Home for Christmas • Rockin' Around the Christmas Tree • Silver Bells • and more.

00416721	Book only	$6.99
00416722	Book/CD	$12.99

CLASSICS
arr. Randall Hartsell

11 solos: Bridal Chorus (Wagner) • Can-Can (Offenbach) • A Little Night Music (Mozart) • Lullaby (Brahms) • Ode to Joy (Beethoven) • Swan Lake (Tchaikovsky) • and more.

00406550	Book only	$5.99
00406736	Book/CD	$10.99

DISNEY TUNES
arr. Glenda Austin

10 delightful Disney songs: The Bare Necessities • Candle on the Water • Kiss the Girl • Mickey Mouse March • Winnie the Pooh • Zip-A-Dee-Doo-Dah • and more.

00416748	Book only	$6.99
00416749	Book/CD	$12.99

FAMILIAR TUNES
arr. Glenda Austin

17 solos, including: Bingo • Buffalo Gals • If You're Happy and You Know It • I'm a Little Teapot • Lightly Row • Polly Put the Kettle On • Take Me Out to the Ball Game • and more.

00406457	Book only	$5.99
00406740	Book/CD	$10.99

HYMNS
arr. Mary K. Sallee

11 hymns: Amazing Grace • Faith of Our Fathers • For the Beauty of the Earth • Holy, Holy, Holy • Jesus Loves Me • Jesus Loves the Little Children • What a Friend We Have in Jesus • and more.

00406413	Book only	$5.99
00406731	Book/CD	$10.99

SONGS FROM MANY LANDS
arr. Carolyn C. Setliff

10 piano solos: Beautiful Dreamer • The Blue Bells of Scotland • Cielito Lindo • Du, Du, Liegst Mir im Herzen • Jasmine Flower • Little White Dove • 'O Sole Mio • On the Shore Across the Lake • Song of the Seasons • Sur le Pont d'Avignon.

00416682	Book only	$5.99
00416683	Book/CD	$10.99

Also available:

AMERICAN TUNES
arr. Eric Baumgartner

00406753	Book only	$5.99
00406792	Book/CD	$10.99

BLUES AND BOOGIE
Carolyn Miller

00406539	Book only	$5.99
00406727	Book/CD	$10.99

BROADWAY SONGS
arr. Carolyn Miller

00416926	Book only	$6.99
00416927	Book/CD	$12.99

CHRISTMAS CAROLS
arr. Carolyn Miller

00406391	Book only	$5.99
00406722	Book/CD	$10.99

CHRISTMAS CLASSICS
arr. Eric Baumgartner

00416825	Book only	$6.99
00416824	Book/CD	$12.99

EASY DUETS
arr. Carolyn Miller

00416830	Book only	$5.99
00416831	Book/CD	$10.99

JAZZ AND ROCK
Eric Baumgartner

00406572	Book only	$5.99
00406718	Book/CD	$10.99

JEWISH FAVORITES
arr. Eric Baumgartner

00416532	Book only	$5.99
00416670	Book/CD	$10.99

RECITAL PIECES
Carolyn Miller

00416539	Book only	$5.99
00416672	Book/CD	$10.99

EXCLUSIVELY DISTRIBUTED BY

WILLIS MUSIC

HAL•LEONARD®
CORPORATION
7777 W. BLUEMOUND RD. P.O. BOX 13819
MILWAUKEE, WISCONSIN 53213

Complete song lists online at **www.halleonard.com**
Prices, contents, and availability subject to change without notice.